HOW TO PLAY LIKE A PRO

FOOTBALL SKILLS

BY MARTY GITLIN

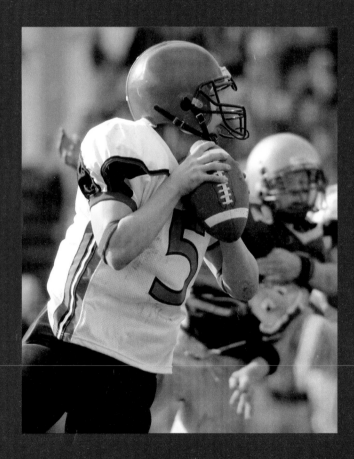

Enslow Elementary
an imprint of
Enslow Publishers, Inc.
40 Industrial Road
Box 398
Berkeley Heights, NJ 07922
USA

http://www.enslow.com

Enslow Elementary, an imprint of Enslow Publishers, Inc.

Enslow Elementary® is a registered trademark of Enslow Publishers, Inc.

Library of Congress Cataloging-in-Publication Data
Gitlin, Marty.
  Football skills : how to play like a pro / Martin Gitlin.
      p. cm. — (How to play like a pro)
  Summary: "Readers will learn how to throw a football, make and receive handoffs, run play patterns, play defense and many other football skills in this book"—Provided by publisher.
  Includes bibliographical references and index.
  ISBN-13: 978-0-7660-3203-3
  1. Football—Training—Juvenile literature. I. Title.
  GV953.5.G58 2009
  796.332—dc22
                                    2007048514

Credits
Editorial Direction: Red Line Editorial, Inc.
Cover & interior design: Becky Daum
Editors: Bob Temple, Dave McMahon
Special thanks to Steve Trivisonno, head football coach at Mentor (Ohio) High School, for his help with this book.

Printed in the United States of America

10 9 8 7 6 5 4 3 2

Photo credits: AP Photo/Chris Carlson, 4; AP Photo/David Zalubowski, 7, 15, 21; AP Photo/Scott Audette, 8; AP/Michael Conroy, 9, 37; iStockPhoto/Crystal Chatham, 10; AP Photo/Matt Slocum, 11; iStockPhoto/Bill Grove, 12, 16, 26, 29; AP/Jeff T. Green, 13; AP/David Duprey, 17, 31; AP/John Froschauer, 18; iStockPhoto/Hasan Shaheed, 19; iStockPhoto/James Boulette, 20, 34; AP/David J. Phillip, 22; iStockPhoto/Mike Strasinger, 23; AP/Nam Y. Huh, 25; AP Photo/John Raoux, 27; AP/Chris Gardner, 28; iStockPhoto/Jane Norton, 32; AP/Alan Diaz, 33; AP Photo/Marcio Jose Sanchez, 35; iStockPhoto/Daniel Padavona, 36; iStockPhoto/Matt Matthews, 38; AP/Keith Sarokcic, 39; AP/Tom Gannam, 41 (top); iStockPhoto/Curtis J. Morley, 41 (bottom); AP/Bill Kostroun, 42; AP Photo/Mark Duncan, 43; iStockPhoto/Amy Myers, 44; AP Photo/Wade Payne, 45.

Cover Photo: iStockPhoto/Bill Grove (large image); AP Photo/Julie Jacobson (small image)

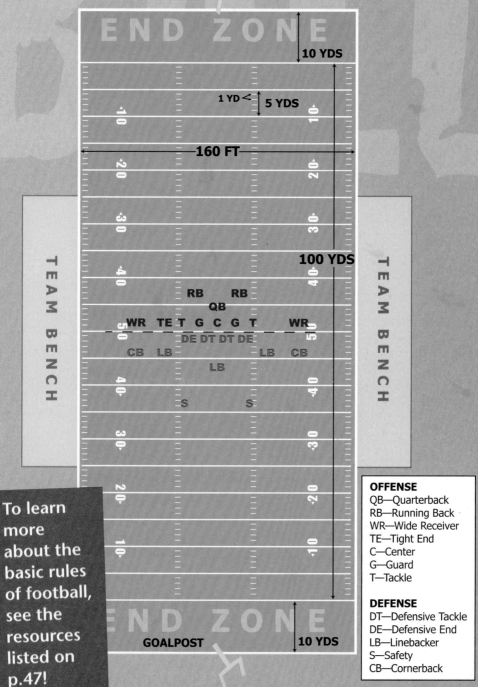

GOALPOST

E N D   Z O N E

10 YDS

1 YD
5 YDS

160 FT

100 YDS

RB   RB
QB
WR   TE T G C G T   WR
DE DT DT DE
CB   LB   LB   CB
LB
S   S

E N D   Z O N E

GOALPOST

10 YDS

To learn more about the basic rules of football, see the resources listed on p.47!

OFFENSE
QB—Quarterback
RB—Running Back
WR—Wide Receiver
TE—Tight End
C—Center
G—Guard
T—Tackle

DEFENSE
DT—Defensive Tackle
DE—Defensive End
LB—Linebacker
S—Safety
CB—Cornerback

TEAM BENCH

TEAM BENCH

PASSING

Passes can travel 60 yards, one foot, or anywhere in between. No matter how far they are thrown, passes are exciting plays.

The quarterback receives the ball from the center. He then throws it to another player—usually, a wide receiver, tight end, or running back. If the quarterback's intended receiver catches the ball, the ball is placed at the spot where the receiver is tackled or goes out of bounds. If it is not caught, the ball returns to the spot at which the play began.

Any time a defensive player catches the ball, it is called an interception. The defensive team takes over. This is known as a turnover. Passing is an important part of the offense.

Who can pass?

The quarterback is not always the passer. Running backs and receivers are also eligible to throw forward passes. Teams do this to try to confuse the defense. Usually, however, the quarterback makes most of the passing attempts.

Most teams have one quarterback who plays the entire game. But every team in high school, college, and pro football has more than one quarterback on its roster.

Touchdown!

The sweetest sight for offensive players is a referee raising his arms in the air. That is the signal for a touchdown. When a passing play ends in a touchdown being scored, it is called a touchdown pass. Even if a receiver catches a short pass and runs into the end zone, it is still considered a touchdown pass.

In his first year as a starting quarterback, David Garrard threw eighteen touchdown passes and only three interceptions. Garrard, who plays for the Jacksonville Jaguars of the National Football League, also passed for 2,509 yards in the regular season.

THROWING THE BALL

There are several steps to throwing a football. After receiving the ball from the center, the quarterback drops back a few steps to allow space for his blockers to work. He grips the ball with three fingers on the back half of the laces. The index finger is behind the laces.

As the quarterback surveys the receivers and defense, he decides quickly where to throw the ball. He brings his arm back just behind his ear and follows through toward the target as the ball is released. Depending on how far the pass needs to go, it can be a straighter throw or have more loft. Passes thrown with more loft are better for longer distances.

Practice

Find two friends to help you. Have one run different pass patterns. He will be your receiver. Have the other friend cover him as he runs the routes. He will be the defensive back. Try throwing the ball to your receiver without the defensive back knocking it away or intercepting it.

PASSING

His arm is pulled back and prepared to throw the ball forward.

Wait until the last second to look at the receiver to avoid giving away the play.

His throwing hand is placed over the back half of the ball with the tips of three fingers across the laces. The index finger is behind the laces while the thumb grips the other side of the ball.

His weight is balanced as he prepares to throw.

Record Setter

Peyton Manning of the Indianapolis Colts threw at least twenty-five touchdown passes in each of his first ten seasons. He was the MVP of the 2007 Super Bowl.

His back foot is planted and the front foot takes a step forward just before the release.

RUNNING THE OFFENSE

Why is the quarterback often the star of the team? Because nearly every offensive play begins when he receives the football. His ability to find an open receiver and to throw the ball on target is critical to the success of his offense. A quarterback must be able to throw short, medium, and long passes. They must be on target and easy to catch. He must have a strong arm to reach his targets

quickly but also a soft touch on shorter passes to make them easy to catch.

Leadership is an important quality for a quarterback. So is the ability to direct a team into the end zone for touchdowns. The confidence of his team-mates is essential.

Practice

Set up five targets in your backyard. Throw a football at one of them. Then, run as fast as you can to pick up the football, and throw it to the next target. Continue to throw until you've hit all five targets. This will improve your skills in running an offense with the clock winding down.

Audibles

Sometimes, the quarterback decides to change the play at the line of scrimmage, where the ball sits on the ground. This is called an "audible." Some teams use hand signals to call the new play. Other teams use key words, which the quarterback calls out.

Fool the Defense

The best passing game is one that keeps the defensive players guessing. Throwing a pass when a defense is expecting a run can catch the defense unaware. A good quarterback won't look at his target until the last second.

Dallas Cowboys quarterback Tony Romo called audibles on the way to passing for 4,211 yards and thirty-six touchdowns during the 2007 regular season.

HANDING THE BALL OFF

The quarterback almost always receives the ball from the center, but doesn't always throw it. He often hands the ball to a running back. For a proper handoff as a quarterback, take a step back, turn sideways, and plant the ball firmly into the running back's belly. The handoff to the running back needs perfect timing. The quarterback must release the ball just as the runner is taking it. If the handoff is not made cleanly, the ball could be fumbled away to the opponent.

Practice

Have a friend line up behind you like a running back. Hold a ball out in front of you, as if you are receiving the center snap. Call out, "Hike!" and have your friend rush forward to receive the handoff. Turn and place the ball into his belly as he goes by. Try to become as smooth as you can by repeating it over and over.

PASSING

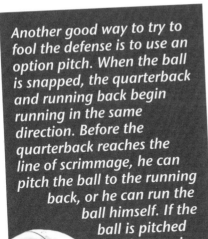

Another good way to try to fool the defense is to use an option pitch. When the ball is snapped, the quarterback and running back begin running in the same direction. Before the quarterback reaches the line of scrimmage, he can pitch the ball to the running back, or he can run the ball himself. If the ball is pitched to the running back, it must be pitched backward.

Watch the Fake!

To fool a team's defense, a running back can throw the ball instead of running with it. When the running back receives the ball, the defense anticipates a run and charges at him. That often leaves receivers open to catch a pass from the running back.

Play Action

A fake handoff is often used to disguise a passing play. This type of play is called a play-action fake.

RUSHING & RECEIVING

It only makes sense that the rushing game revolves around the running backs and the receiving game focuses on the receivers. Running backs receive the ball from the quarterback and try to carry it as far downfield as possible. The blockers attempt to open up a hole in the defense big enough for the backs to run through.

Offenses are able to use a variety of running plays. Some are geared for the running back to run around the end of the line, and others are designed for him to run up the middle. Receivers line up on either side of the line and run certain patterns to try to get open. They try to catch the ball thrown by the quarterback.

Scrambling

The quarterback often runs the ball, too. He might run to escape defensive behemoths breathing down his neck. Sometimes a play calls for a quarterback to run with the ball. But usually, a quarterback runs because he can't find an open receiver or he is about to be tackled by a defender.

There are two types of running backs. One is the tailback, who most often carries the ball. The other is the fullback, who is usually more responsible for blocking.

Short Yardage

When a team only needs a short gain to get a first down, a running play is usually called. A running back tries to break free from defenders to get enough yardage so that his team can keep possession of the ball.

Adrian Peterson (28) rushed for 1,341 yards on 283 carries for the Minnesota Vikings in 2007. He averaged more than ninety-five yards rushing per game. He was named MVP of the Pro Bowl as a rookie.

TAKING A HANDOFF

To take a handoff, both hands should be parallel to the ground. The inside arm, or the one closest to the quarterback, should be on top. The elbow should be raised slightly so the ball does not hit it. Lock the ball with the bottom arm to prevent a fumble. Cover one end with the fingers of the top arm and the other with the crook of the elbow. Keep a short arm's-length distance from the quarterback so there is no collision during the handoff process. Continue moving forward after taking the handoff to maintain momentum.

Practice

Take direct handoffs and pitches from a friend while moving forward. Repeat until the ball is consistently received without a bobble or fumble.

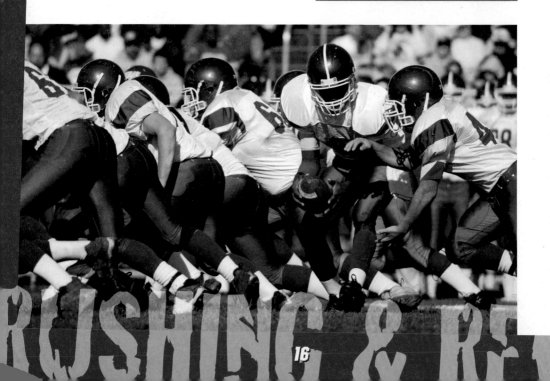

RUSHING & REC

16

End Around

It's rare, but sometimes the wide receiver takes a handoff. This is called an "end around." The receiver races into the backfield from one end of the field and tries to gain ground by running around the other end of the line.

Remember Fakes

If a fake handoff is called, be sure not to try to grab the ball from the quarterback. It could result in a fumble.

His head is up, giving him the ability to look over the defense for possible tacklers.

The most effective way to avoid being tackled in the open field is to keep the head up. Be aware of where defenders are.

The ball is tucked securely against his body with his fingers covering the front tip.

He keeps his body balanced and driving forward, keeping his feet moving.

LT for TDs

LaDainian Tomlinson of the San Diego Chargers scored thirty-one touchdowns in 2006 to break an all-time NFL single-season record.

RUSHING & REC

CARRYING THE BALL

After taking the handoff and breaking through the line of scrimmage, the ball carrier can run with the ball in one arm. Having both hands on the ball at the handoff allows for an easy switch to one hand or the other.

To switch from two hands to one, cover one end of the ball with the fingers, raise the ball to chest level, and lock the other end of the ball into the armpit. Always keep the ball tight to the chest.

Take short, quick strides through the first line of defense. If you are about to get tackled, cover the ball with both hands to protect it.

Practice

Run forward quickly for 10 yards while carrying a football. Practice making sharp cuts to the right and left. Pretend you are avoiding tacklers.

BREAKING TACKLES

Every effort should be made to avoid tackles. Use the arm not holding the ball to fend off defenders. Prevent defenders from securing a strong grasp by pushing them away with the free arm. A quick spin move sometimes works, too. Make sure to keep your balance. Once in the grasp of a defender, keep churning your legs and use every bit of strength to try to break free and keep moving forward. If you are slowed, take high, hard steps to try to get away.

Practice

While wearing full equipment for safety, have a friend try to tackle you while you're carrying the ball. Attempt to escape his grasp by keeping the legs moving.

Listen for the Whistle

Play is stopped when the forward motion of a ball carrier is halted by the defense. Even if he hasn't been tackled, but is in the grasp of one or more defenders, the referee will blow the whistle. The ball will then be placed at that spot on the field.

The quarterback doesn't get as much of a chance to break tackles as do running backs and receivers. Once the quarterback is in the grasp of a defender, the referee will often blow his whistle to stop the play. This is done in an effort to protect the quarterback from injury.

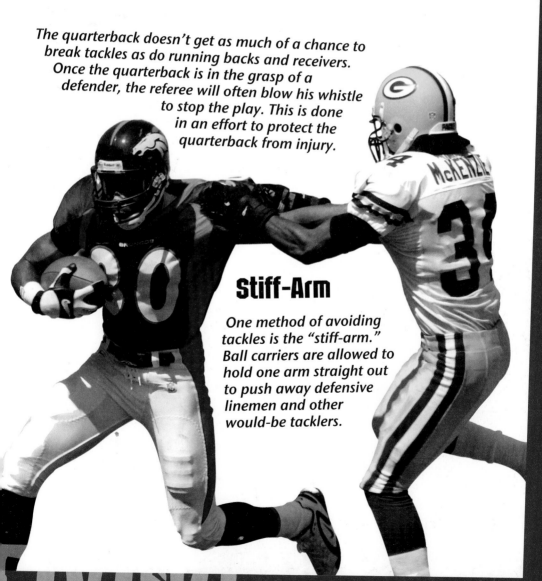

Stiff-Arm

One method of avoiding tackles is the "stiff-arm." Ball carriers are allowed to hold one arm straight out to push away defensive linemen and other would-be tacklers.

CATCHING THE BALL

To catch the ball, move swiftly toward the ball as it gets closer. Keep the arms and hands in front of the body. The knees should be slightly bent with feet spread about two feet apart. The eyes must be constantly on the ball. On a pass coming in above chest level, the elbows should be comfortably bent. To receive the ball, the thumb from the left hand should be touching the thumb from the right hand, and the index finger from the left hand should be touching the index finger from the right hand.

Practice

Have a friend throw the football. Run routes and practice catching the ball while you are moving. Make sure to catch it with your hands. Don't just trap it against your chest with your arms.

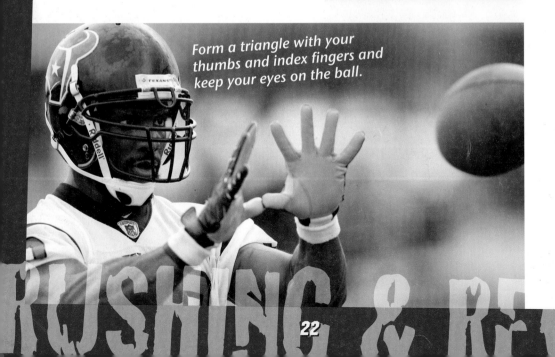

Form a triangle with your thumbs and index fingers and keep your eyes on the ball.

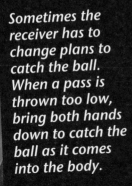

Sometimes the receiver has to change plans to catch the ball. When a pass is thrown too low, bring both hands down to catch the ball as it comes into the body.

All receivers run pass patterns in an attempt to get open. These are called "routes." The length of the routes can be short, medium, or long. Among the most common is the "post pattern," in which a receiver runs straight forward, then cuts at an angle toward the goal post.

BLOCKING

Blockers don't often shine in the spotlight, but they are just as important as any other offensive player. The passing and running plays cannot be successful without good blocking. Blocking is the key to preventing defensive players from reaching ball carriers and quarterbacks. Blocking opens up holes for ball carriers. It also protects quarterbacks, giving them time to find receivers and throw the ball.

The five offensive linemen are the most important blockers. Offensive linemen provide the pivotal blocks, but every offensive player is called on to block sometimes. The offensive line performs as a united group. The most effective offensive lines often consist of players who have played together for a long period of time.

Practice

Bend forward at the waist. Get into a "three point stance" by resting the fingers of one hand on the ground. Pretend a play is starting and push forward as quickly as possible. Repeat often to develop your quickness.

Offensive linemen are often looking for a pancake. No, not to eat! A "pancake block" is achieved when a defender is taken off his feet and lands on his back.

Stay in Front

Because of the risk of injury, blockers are not allowed to hit a defender in the back. Always face the player you plan to block. Blocking a player from behind can result in a "clipping" penalty.

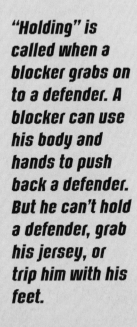

"Holding" is called when a blocker grabs on to a defender. A blocker can use his body and hands to push back a defender. But he can't hold a defender, grab his jersey, or trip him with his feet.

RUN BLOCKING

Footwork and balance are the most important parts of good blocking on running plays. Being strong enough to block a defender out of the way will open up space for the running back. Blockers use positioning and strength to push against the front of the defensive players. Blockers work with other blockers to push away defenders that are getting close to making a tackle. Keep the body low to the ground in the three-point stance before the ball is snapped.

Practice

Line up across from one friend and in front of another. Flip the ball between your legs to the friend behind you and have him run with it. Try to block the other friend to the right or left to clear a path.

Most run blocking by offensive linemen is done by pushing forward. But some plays call for offensive linemen to move quickly to the side and lead a running back around the end of the line, blocking along the way. This play is called a "sweep."

Pass blockers are sometimes turned into run blockers on the same play. If there are no open receivers, the quarterback will often try to run with the ball. The blockers must then try to push defenders back to create room for the quarterback.

He is keeping his eyes on the defensive player to prevent him from making a quick move to get away.

His arms are locked. He's not using his hands to grab the defender.

10 Straight

Jonathan Ogden (75) of the Baltimore Ravens was chosen to play in the Pro Bowl (the NFL all-star game) 10 years in a row. He was named to the American Football Conference team from 1998–2007.

His hips are in front of the defensive player.

His legs continue to move forward as he pushes his body through the defender.

BLOCKING

28

PASS BLOCKING

Protect that quarterback! The main goal of pass blocking is to provide time and space for the quarterback to throw the ball. On running plays, blockers push defenders back. Pass blockers attempt to keep defenders away until the quarterback is able to pass the ball. Do this by stepping back and blocking the defender for several seconds.

Proper footwork is very important in pass blocking. Don't lean backward or stand straight up. While staying balanced, shift your weight slightly forward. This will allow you to have the mobility needed to keep the defenders away from the passer.

Practice

Line up across from one friend and in front of another. Flip the ball between your legs to the friend behind you and have him stand with the ball for five seconds. Meanwhile, try to keep the other friend from reaching the quarterback. See how long your block lasts.

DEFENSE

Offensive players often make the TV highlight shows, but it's difficult to win a game without a strong defense. The two basic forms of defense are pass defense and run defense. An effective pass defense puts pressure on the quarterback before he can throw the ball. The goal is to sack him—tackle him behind the line of scrimmage—or force him to hurry his passes.

Pass coverage is also important. Linebackers and defensive backs are responsible for covering receivers to prevent them from catching the ball.

The goal in run defense is to target the ball carrier and tackle him. The run defense tries to stop the ball carrier as quickly as possible.

Practice

A game of two-hand touch with friends is a good, safe way to practice football skills. Make two teams for a football game. Instead of tackling, however, a player is considered "down" when he is touched by both hands of a defensive player.

One position responsible for both run and pass defense is linebacker. Three or four linebackers position themselves behind the defensive line. They react to tackle a ball carrier on a running play or to cover receivers on a passing play.

The Secondary

Defensive backs form the "secondary," or back line of the defense. There are generally four players in the secondary: a free safety, a strong safety, and two cornerbacks. The cornerbacks are responsible for defending the sidelines, and the safeties patrol the middle of the field. The safeties are often the fastest players on the defense.

Brian Urlacher of the Chicago Bears (54) is known as one of the toughest linebackers in the NFL. The best tacklers wrap up the ball carrier with both arms.

TAKING ON BLOCKERS

Escape and pursue! That is the mission when taking on blockers. Try to escape blockers and pursue, or chase, the ball carrier or quarterback. Footwork and quickness are critical to get away from blockers. One way to avoid a blocker is to take a quick step to one side, then rush quickly to the other side of the blocker. Plant an arm either over or under the arms of the blocker and push through to get the blocker off balance. Strength is also a key element. A defender who is stronger than the blocker will almost always have an advantage. The stronger defender can get to the ball carrier by simply pushing away the blocker.

Practice

Line up directly across from a friend. Put a ball on the ground, several feet behind your friend. Say "hike" and try to get past your friend and to the ball. If you can do that in three seconds or less, you are the winner. If not, your friend wins.

The best defensive players are often double-teamed by blockers. This forces a defender to fight off two blockers instead of one. It often gives another defender an easier path to the ball carrier or quarterback, however.

Blockers can sometimes be avoided completely. Linebackers and defensive backs often try to surprise the offense by running a "blitz." Right at the start of the play, they rush past blockers, trying to reach the quarterback before the ball is thrown.

MAKING A TACKLE

Tackling requires the use of speed and strength to take the ball carrier to the ground. Always keep your head up and keep your eyes on the ball carrier when pursuing him. Never slow down when the target is reached. Keep your head to the side of the ball carrier's body that the ball is on, and drive forward.

Grab the ball carrier's waist or thighs. It is much harder to secure a ball carrier by the upper body because that allows him to continue to churn his legs and break away. Once the ball carrier is in your grasp, pull him toward your body and drive him to the ground.

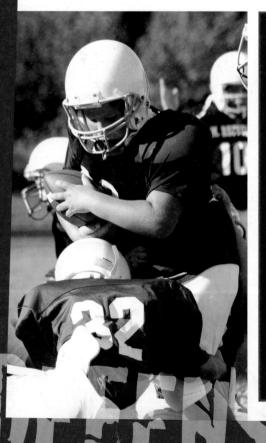

Practice

Stand five feet in front of a friend who is holding the ball. Have him move forward. Attempt to grab him below the waist and tackle him before he can get by. This drill is especially helpful when done slowly. Make sure the ball carrier is holding the ball properly, and place your head to the side where he is carrying the ball. Always wear full equipment.

Facemasking

Due to the risk of injury to the ball carrier, defenders are not allowed to grab the facemask on the helmet when tackling a ball carrier. In fact, no player can grab another player's facemask. This rule violation will cause the referee to call a penalty on the player who grabs the facemask.

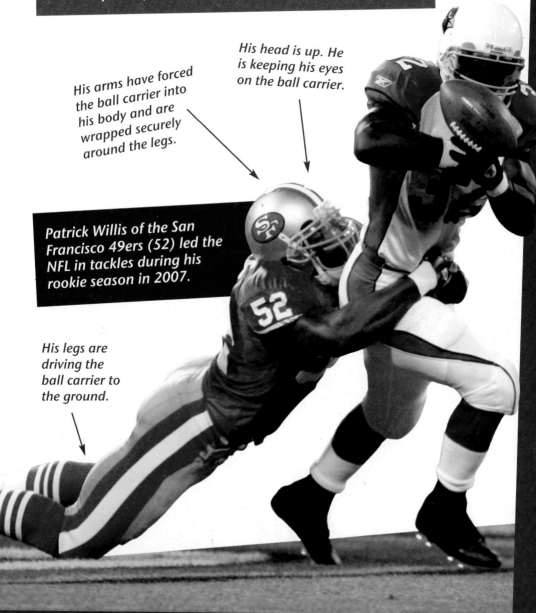

His head is up. He is keeping his eyes on the ball carrier.

His arms have forced the ball carrier into his body and are wrapped securely around the legs.

Patrick Willis of the San Francisco 49ers (52) led the NFL in tackles during his rookie season in 2007.

His legs are driving the ball carrier to the ground.

MAN-TO-MAN COVERAGE

One of the most difficult tasks in football is covering a receiver. It takes great footwork and quickness. When lining up across from a receiver, bend slightly forward, with the chest over the toes. If the receiver runs straight forward, backpedal quickly. Take short, quick steps. Then turn to the receiver and remain with him. Be aware of body fakes by the receiver. Make sure he really is heading in a certain direction. Stay with him. If a defender loses one full step to the receiver, he is beaten. If he does fall behind, he should sprint as fast as he can to catch up.

Don't watch the quarterback. Stay with the receiver until he reaches his hands up for a thrown ball. If you can, knock the ball away before it reaches the receiver. If the ball gets into his hands, try to strip it away.

Practice

Assign one friend to be the quarterback. Have him plan pass routes with another friend. Try to cover the receiver as closely as possible and prevent him from catching the ball.

Who Covers?

Cornerbacks and safeties aren't the only defensive players responsible for man-to-man pass coverage. When a quarterback drops back to pass, one or two linebackers generally shadow the tight end or running backs who are trying to get open.

Chucking

Defensive players are allowed to push or bump a receiver within five yards of the line. This is called "chucking." Receivers can't be touched again unless you are trying to catch the ball.

ZONE COVERAGE

When a defense is playing in a zone, players are responsible for certain areas of the field rather than for particular receivers. Defensive backs and sometimes linebackers will stay in their zones. They cover any players who enter that area of the field. Defenders must have confidence that their teammates will handle other areas of the field. Defenders should never leave a zone to cover a receiver until the ball is actually thrown. The quarterback could fake a pass, and the defender could run into the zone where he thinks the ball is going. That would leave the defender's zone open.

Practice

Have a friend play quarterback and another friend play receiver. Stand at least twenty feet in front of the quarterback. Have the receiver run at least ten feet away from you to receive a pass. When the ball is thrown, react quickly. Run as fast as possible to try to knock the ball away.

Matchups

One goal of an offensive team is to get a fast receiver matched up against a slower defender. Sometimes offenses will run plays that force a linebacker to cover a speedy receiver. Zone defenses often prevent such matchups like these, where the receiver has an advantage on the slower linebacker.

Intercepting

Never run in front of a receiver to try for an interception unless you are certain the ball can be reached. If the ball gets behind a defender, he is out of position. Then it is more difficult to knock the ball away from the receiver or tackle the receiver after the ball is caught. It also often leaves the receiver with plenty of room to run.

A four-time Pro Bowl selection, Pittsburgh Steelers safety Troy Polamalu is one of the most exciting defensive backs in the game. He once intercepted a pass and ran toward the opponent's end zone before a defender pulled him down by his hair!

SPECIAL TEAMS

For most of the game, either the offense or the defense is on the field. But special teams are just as important. They take the field during kickoffs, punts, and field-goal attempts.

Kickers and punters have specific skills that make them vital to the success of the team. A long kickoff can help pin an opponent deep in its own territory. By contrast, a punt returner can use the help of blockers in front of him to give the offense momentum. A great field-goal kicker can win games in the closing minutes of play.

Practice

Get a kicking tee or have a friend hold the ball for you. Place the ball with one point down and tilted slightly back toward you. Take about five steps back. Run up to the ball and kick it. For greatest distance, hit the ball with the top of the foot, not the toe. Attempt to boot the ball through a target about ten yards away. Increase the distance as your kicks grow stronger and more accurate.

In order for a kickoff to be legal, no players on the kickoff team can cross the kickoff line before the ball is booted.

The opposing players will often try to block a punt, but they must be careful! If they make contact with the kicker without touching the ball, they are penalized for "roughing the kicker." Then the kicking team gets to keep possession of the ball.

PUNTING & KICKING

When punting, don't grip the ball too tightly or too loosely! The punter holds the ball with the laces up, out in front of the body. Place the right hand on the bottom right of the ball and the left hand on the top left. Take one small step forward with the kicking foot. Then take two regular steps and drop the ball straight down to the kicking foot. Kick the ball when it lands between the toe and instep and follow the leg through. The leg should extend as high as it can comfortably reach.

Big Leg

Most professional kickers average at least forty yards a punt. The distance is not judged from the point of the kick, but from the line of scrimmage, where the ball is snapped. Another way is to time how long it remains in the air before it is caught. This is known as "hang time."

SPECIAL TEAMS

His head is down to make sure he keeps his eyes on the ball.

His arms are bent slightly forward to keep his body balanced.

Placekicking is used in kicking field goals. The ball is snapped to a holder, who places the ball on the field. The placekicker then tries to kick the ball between the goal posts and above the crossbar at the end of the field. If successful, his team gets three points. Placekicking can also earn an extra point after a touchdown.

His leg creates force to provide plenty of distance

Super Kicker

Adam Vinatieri of the Indianapolis Colts has been the starting placekicker for four Super Bowl champions, including the Colts and the New England Patriots.

His foot is moving swiftly and strongly through the ball.

Blocking for a kick returner is different than run or pass blocking. The object is to take a defender out of the play. This is done by knocking the defender off his feet with a quick push. Blocking on a kickoff or punt return is done in the open field, away from the line of scrimmage and with defenders running at full speed. On kick returns, blockers run down the field in a "lane." They are responsible for blocking all defenders in their lanes. To block one defender, the blocker ties up a defender long enough for the ball carrier to pass him.

The goal for the blocker is to knock down a defender immediately. Next, the blocker should find another defender to block if the play has not ended.

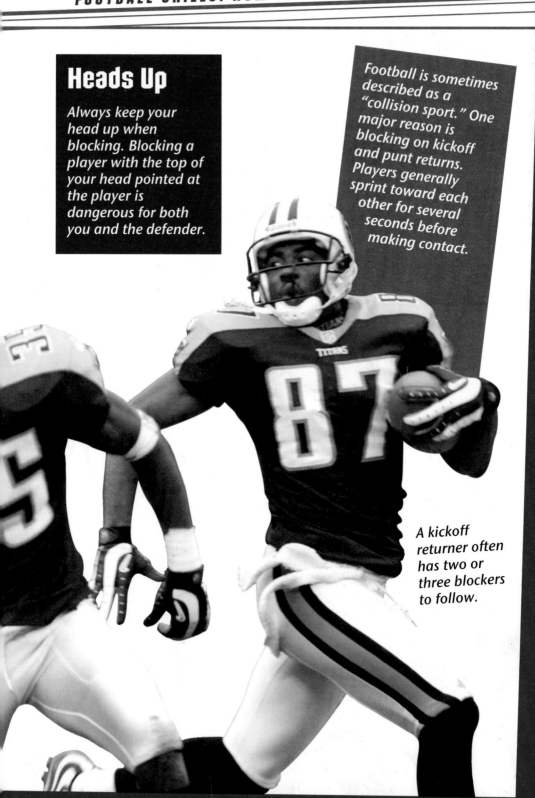

Heads Up

Always keep your head up when blocking. Blocking a player with the top of your head pointed at the player is dangerous for both you and the defender.

Football is sometimes described as a "collision sport." One major reason is blocking on kickoff and punt returns. Players generally sprint toward each other for several seconds before making contact.

A kickoff returner often has two or three blockers to follow.

GLOSSARY

★ **blocker**—An offensive player who pushes a defender to keep him away from a ball carrier.

★ **defensive back**—One of four players primarily responsible for covering receivers and preventing them from catching the ball.

★ **defensive lineman**—One of three or four players primarily responsible for pursuing and tackling running backs and quarterbacks.

★ **fumble**—The loss of control of the football by a ball carrier. Possession of the ball is given to whichever team gets control of the loose ball.

★ **handoff**—To give the ball to a teammate. Usually, this involves a quarterback handing it to a running back.

★ **interception**—A forward pass caught by a member of the defensive team.

★ **linebacker**—One of four defenders who plays behind the defensive linemen and is responsible for both run and pass coverage.

★ **placekicker**—The player who kicks the ball off a tee on a kickoff to start a game or half, or off the ground from the grasp of a holder for a field goal.

★ **punter**—The player who kicks the ball away after his team gives up possession of the ball.

★ **quarterback**—The offensive leader who takes the ball on a snap from the center at the start of each play. The quarterback either hands it off, throws it, or runs with it.

★ **receiver**—Any offensive player who catches the ball, including a running back, wide receiver, or tight end.

★ **touchdown**—A scoring play, worth six points, in which a player reaches the opponent's end zone with the ball.

LEARN MORE

INTERNET ADDRESSES

★ *About.com: Football*
http://football.about.com/od/football101/Football_101.htm

★ *American Youth Football (AYF)*
http://www.americanyouthfootball.com

★ *Pop Warner*
http://www.popwarner.com

★ *USA Football*
http://www.usafootball.com

BOOKS & VIDEOS

★ *101 Defensive Stunts for Youth Football,* by Chris Booth. Monterey, CA: Coaches Choice, 2008.

★ *101 Youth Football Plays,* by Chris Booth. Monterey, CA: Coaches Choice, 2007.

★ *Defensive Football Strategies,* by American Football Coaches Association. Champaign, IL: Human Kinetics, 2000.

★ *Football Skills and Drills,* by Thomas Bass. Champaign, IL: Human Kinetics, 2004.

★ *Fundamentals of Youth Football (video),* by Jeff Scurran. Tucson, AZ: Sport Videos, 2004.

INDEX